Amazon FBA

A Comprehensive Guide to Start Selling Private Label Products on Amazon

Braden Nardelli

©2016

©Copyright 2016

By Braden Nardelli - *All rights reserved.*

This document is geared towards providing exact and reliable information in regards to the topic and issue covered. The publication is sold with the idea that the publisher is not required to render accounting, officially permitted, or otherwise, qualified services. If advice is necessary, legal or professional, a practiced individual in the profession should be ordered.

From a Declaration of Principles which was accepted and approved equally by a Committee of the American Bar Association and a Committee of Publishers and Associations.

In no way is it legal to reproduce, duplicate, or transmit any part of this document in either electronic means or in printed format. Recording of this publication is strictly prohibited and any storage of this document is not allowed unless with written permission from the publisher. All rights reserved.

The information provided herein is stated to be truthful and consistent, in that any liability, in terms of inattention or otherwise, by any usage or abuse of any policies, processes, or directions contained within is the solitary and utter responsibility of the recipient reader. Under no circumstances will any legal responsibility or blame be held against the publisher for any reparation, damages, or monetary loss due to the information herein, either directly or indirectly.

Respective authors own all copyrights not held by the publisher.

The information herein is offered for informational purposes solely, and is universal as so. The presentation of the information is without contract or any type of guarantee assurance.

The trademarks that are used are without any consent, and the publication of the trademark is without permission or backing by the trademark owner. All trademarks and brands within this book are for clarifying purposes only and are the owned by the owners themselves, not affiliated with this document.

Disclaimer and Terms of Use

The Author and Publisher has strived to be as accurate and complete as possible in the creation of this book, notwithstanding the fact that he does not warrant or represent at any time that the contents within are accurate due to the rapidly changing nature of the Internet.

While all attempts have been made to verify information provided in this publication, the Author and Publisher assumes no responsibility for errors, omissions, or contrary interpretation of the subject matter herein.

Any perceived slights of specific persons, peoples, or organizations are unintentional. In practical advice books, like anything else in life, there are no guarantees of results. Readers are cautioned to rely on their own judgment about their individual circumstances and act accordingly.

This book is not intended for use as a source of legal, medical, business, accounting or financial advice. All readers are advised to seek services of competent professionals in the legal, medical, business, accounting, and finance fields.

Introduction

I want to thank you and congratulate you for buying the book, *"A Comprehensive Guide to Start Selling Private Label Products on Amazon"*.

This book contains proven steps and strategies on how to Start Selling Private Label Product on Amazon.

This guide is aimed at anyone who is looking to make money through Amazon or wants to learn how to make the most of Amazon's website. By the end of this guide you should be well acquainted with how to sell items with Amazon, how to purchase items and where to find the best deals on Amazon.

Thanks again for buying this book, I hope you enjoy it!

CONTENTS

- Chapter 1 1
- What is Private Labelling? 1
- The History of Private Label 4
- How You Can Share in Amazon's Global Success and Make Money From Fulfillment by Amazon 9
- Chapter 2 23
- Private Label Rights Market Research 23
- Steps for private labelling on Amazon 28
- Best Private Label Products to Sell on Amazon ... 40
- Chapter 3 49
- How Much Could You Earn With a Private-Label Business? 49
- Some lucrative Amazon FBA Private Label Product Ideas 51
- How To Find Suppliers & Manufacturers Fast 53
- Chapter 4 63
- Uses and usefulness of private 63
- Private Label Categories 68
- Conclusion 73

Chapter 1 : What is Private Labelling?

A private label product is manufactured by Company A, but with the brand name (i.e., logo and packaging) of Company B. In theory, Company A (the producer) provides a ready-made 'product template', to which other buyers can apply their own brands.

A private label product is manufactured by a contract or third-party manufacturer and sold under a retailer's brand name. As the retailer, you specify everything about the product – what goes in it, how it's packaged, what the label looks like – and pay to have it produced and delivered to your store. This is in contrast to buying products from other companies with their brand names on them.

For example, Target sells a variety of branded snacks from companies like General Mills and Frito-

Lay, but it also sell its own chips and crackers under the Archer Farms brand – Target's private label brand.

Hair salons often create their own branded line of shampoos, conditioners, and styling products for their customers to buy and take home. Restaurants often decide to private label condiments or mixes that have become popular with customers. Maid services could private label a line of household cleaners and pet stores could private label a line of pet foods and grooming tools.

Growing market shares and increasing variety of private label consumer packaged goods is now a global phenomenon. However, private label market shares exhibit widespread diversity across international markets and product categories. Empirical research on private label products has been of substantial interest to both marketing academics and managers. Considerable work has been done on well-defined areas of private-label research such as private-label brand strategy, market performance of private-label products, competition with national brands, market structure, and buyer behavior.

For example, Richelieu Foods is a private-label company producing frozen pizza, salad dressing, marinades, and condiments for other companies, including Hy-Vee, Aldi, Save-A-Lot, Sam's Club, Hannaford Brothers Co, BJ's Wholesale Club (Earth's Pride brand) and Shaw's Supermarkets (Culinary Circle brand). Another example is the Cott Corporation, which manufactures private-label beverages for supermarket chains. McBride plc is a Europe-based provider of private-label household and personal care products.

The benefit of private labelling is that you can create a branded product, without investing into all too much time and money in product development – and tooling. Hence, you can launch a product much faster.

Again, this is all theory, and I will explain later why this is not really how it works out in reality. But, the point is still valid.

With all that said, branding is still a key for startups and small businesses, as these cannot compete on pricing. This is especially obvious on marketplaces, such as Amazon.com.

The History of Private Label

Private-label products or services, also known as "phantom brands", are typically those manufactured or provided by one company for offer under another company's brand. Private-label goods and services are available in a wide range of industries from food to cosmetics to web hosting. They are often positioned as lower-cost alternatives to regional, national or international brands, although recently some private label brands have been positioned as "premium" brands to compete with existing "name" brands.

For over a century, consumer packaged goods (CPG) manufacturers have dominated brand innovation, formulating products and driving consumer motivation for purchase, while retailers have served as the real estate managers governing where these new products are sold. Essentially, CPGs invented and retailers stocked the shelf. This approach became so integrated that through the concept of category champions, CPGs took control of retailers' merchandising strategies – and in some cases drove store layout. But as this model evolved, the more progressive retailers began packing products under their own brands and the industry of "private label" was born.

Private label was initially successful due to the simple proposition of value alternative. For individuals shopping on a budget or for higher income shoppers in low involvement categories, private label provided an attractive price point. This concept flourished, as it not only provided incremental revenue for the retailer via better margins, but it also positioned the competing CPG offerings as more innovative and of higher quality, thereby substantiating the price premium at which they still operate today.

Private label has grown more sophisticated over the years. Noticing the margin opportunity in converting CPG sales to PL sales, retailers began creating dedicated teams to help manage and build their private-label business. This business now comprises two distinct but simultaneous strategies. The first involves a three-tiered approach to value alternatives: opening price point (value), mid-tier (national brand equivalent/NBE, e.g. Oreos) and premium tier (also NBE, e.g. Pepperidge Farm). The second strategy introduces "opportunistic category brands," which are created and launched into specific categories where the tiered strategy either has a limited potential for success or just doesn't get permission from the consumer.

This is essentially how the private label industry has worked over the last three decades. Once CPG products (or in some cases, new categories) have proved successful, retailers have launched value alternatives. To be fair, in some instances retailers have innovated unique line extensions, flavor options and interesting licensing arrangements. But for the most part, CPGs drove true product innovation. As a rule, the grocery retailer industry norm was to have specific CPG "targets" for their product development teams to work against.

The traditional retail model has evolved notably in the past 30 years, and so has the relationship between consumer packaged goods manufacturers (CPGs) and the businesses who sell their goods. As today's retailers continue to improve the quality of their own brands and gain a greater share of the market, this not only affects the role of manufacturers: this shifting dynamic paves the way for new opportunities for CPGs and retailers to combine their best practices, forging stronger, mutually lucrative affinities.

How You Can Share in Amazon's Global Success and Make Money From Fulfillment by Amazon

The Amazon is only not a retailer, in the real sense on Amazon you can curating your products and can presenting your product to their best advantages to inform and can persuade the customer. They are such a agnostic fulfillment platform that are available, whose goal depth and breadth of information of the customer.

Amazon is the sales marketplace that originally started out as a place to sell books. But in the last decade it's graduated to selling anything and everything... and become one of the biggest brands in the world. Not only that but it's a famous brand that allows - in fact encourages - entrepreneurs to share in their success by selling products right there on Amazon itself.

Over the last couple of years Amazon have been working on another way you can make money in partnership with them. It's called Fulfillment by Amazon.

Making money through Affiliate Marketing, according to todays technology has enabled the people to find some other means of the income. For so many things the internet has just been become a medium way for these things, and social media, particularly, has become so leading and dominant that are finding by the people and can find so many uses out of it.

Affiliate Marketing is the promoting act of the third party products direct through your personal blog or your personal site. It's mainly a beneficial and joint partnership that you as a marketer and the other of the party, usually a owner of a website that will gain for every sale made.

In affiliate marketing, you must can promote your services and your goods against the merchant, and then you can get a commission out of the generated profits by the sale.

How You Can Share in Amazon's Global Success and Make Money from Fulfillment by Amazon

Now to me Fulfillment by Amazon sounds like a really exciting way of making money in the 21st century Internet age. Because it is a business model whereby you can just focus on marketing and making sales. Then have Amazon do all the "hard" physical work of stocking, storing and shipping your products to your customers for you.

You know, Amazon are always something of a puzzle to me! They come out with the latest, cutting-edge business models and invest millions in making them successful. There's no doubt

Amazon's brand image, ordering and distribution systems are absolutely without equal.

Then they let any Tom, Dick or Harriet share them for free. Just why they would let ordinary people take advantage of all this for no up-front cost whatsoever, I don't know! It seems crazy, it doesn't seem to make sense at all, but they do it... and it's almost always a big success.

So I thought it's high time we came back to Amazon and looked at exactly how Fulfillment by Amazon works, whether it is as good as it sounds... and whether it can make some money for you.

Amazon... did you know?

- Amazon attracts 50 million consumers a month worldwide.
- Amazon has been voted the third favourite UK retailer (after John Lewis and IKEA).

- 1.3 million businesses are selling on Amazon.
- Amazon's business grew 18% last year... when most businesses were shrinking.

So, what is Fulfillment by Amazon exactly?

The basic concept of Fulfillment by Amazon, like all Amazon's concepts, is simple... although there are a lot of ins-and-outs which I'll look at later. With this service you send whatever products you want to sell (your inventory as Amazon like to call it) directly to Amazon. Whether it be books, CDs, clothing, computer accessories, toys, or whatever. They store it in their warehouse for you. Then when orders are received Amazon will pick, pack and ship the product directly to your customers for you.

You can use Fulfillment by Amazon whether you just want to sell a few things on Amazon as a sideline or want to sell thousands of products. You can use it if you are starting a new business or have an existing one that you want to change over to Fulfillment by Amazon.

You can use Fulfillment by Amazon to send out things you are selling on Amazon itself or things you are selling elsewhere. This is what Amazon called Multi Channel Fulfillment. One more thing: if you start using Fulfillment by Amazon you don't have to have everything fulfilled by Amazon. You can use it for some products and not others.

Pros and cons

So then, let's have a look at the pros and cons of Fulfillment by Amazon:

Pro. You get to benefit from Amazon's reputation. Amazon is a brand that's trusted by customers worldwide. When they order something that is shipped by Amazon they know they will get it. And fast. And they know they can return it if they want to. This can make a massive difference when they are deciding whether to buy from you.

Pro. You can offer faster service. Amazon has state-of-the-art online order processing and fulfillment operations. Chances are they can get your products to your buyers faster than you can.

Pro. Your products can be ranked higher on Amazon. With an Fulfillment by Amazon item your item shows up at the top of the search more often than not. Products from non-Fulfillment by Amazon sellers are listed by total cost (product price plus shipping) but your items are listed by price only. So often you can price your items close to the lowest total price, maybe be the first item in the list and attract more buyers.

Pro. Your customers can get free delivery. Using Fulfillment by Amazon will mean your customers get free delivery on your products... using Super Saver Delivery or Amazon Prime. That can give you a big advantage over sellers who don't use Fulfillment by Amazon.

Pro. Lower overheads. You'll need to do the figures but, in most cases, there can be good cost savings. With FBA you won't need premises for storage, staff to do picking/shipping and associated admin. It might even mean you can drop your prices, sell more goods and yet still make more profit.

Pro. You can be MUCH more productive. I think this is the biggest potential benefit. When you use FBA you won't need to spend time sorting, warehousing, picking and packing goods. Amazon do it for you. They can also handle customer services, returns, etc.

This means you can spend almost all your time actually marketing and selling - things that make you money. And because you can spend more time doing that you should, at least in theory, be able to make more money.

Now, although Amazon will tell you there aren't any disadvantages to FBA I think there are a few you need to bear in mind:

Con. It's not so good for products that take a long time to sell or which are unproven sellers. Because you have to pay a monthly storage fee for as long as Amazon have your products.

Con. Using FBA might make it difficult to compete with other sellers, especially those also using FBA.

Because how are you going to differentiate your product and your service from theirs?

Con. This is what I think is the main drawback of Fulfillment by Amazon. Your business is almost totally reliant on Amazon.

What if something goes wrong... for example their systems fail and they don't fulfill your orders or lose your stock? Or if they put up their prices?

And what if, after getting your product in an Amazon box, the buyer just decides to go back and buy from Amazon next time?

Getting started with Fulfillment by Amazon

So let's have a look at how you can get started using Fulfillment by Amazon.

At this point I should say that there's tons of detailed information on how it all works at the Amazon website. But that's really hard going and a lot of it is difficult to follow. So here I'm going to try to give you a simple, user-friendly summary of Fulfillment by Amazon.

First of all Fulfillment by Amazon is not separate to the other methods of using Amazon. It is fully integrated with them. You just set up to sell on Amazon Marketplace in the usual way then choose to FBA the products you want to.

It's very easy to get started with Amazon Marketplace. You don't need to register in advance. You can open a seller account when you list your first product. To register as a seller you will need a business name, an address, a display name (which can be your business name or something else), a credit card and a telephone contact number. That's all you need to get started. Go to http://www.amazon.com, scroll down the page to 'Make Money With Us' and then 'Sell On Amazon' to get started.

Amazon offers two ways of selling - informally called 'selling a little' or 'selling a lot'.

Basically 'a little' is for occasional and hobby sellers who expect to sell less than 35 items a month. It costs $1 plus a referral fee for each sale and you can't sell in all the Amazon categories. Selling 'a lot' is for businesses who expect to sell more than 35 items a month. You pay a $35 monthly fixed fee and a referral fee. You can sell in all the Amazon product categories. The 'selling a little' option isn't really for use with Fulfillment by Amazon.

To use Fulfillment by Amazon fully you will also really need to become what Amazon call a Pro Merchant Seller. Pro Merchants have access to volume selling and bulk listing tools. There is a web interface that can allows you to more easily manage your descriptions of the products, inventory and orders. You will also be able to export and import information to and from your account. Normally the Pro Merchant option will work out much cheaper and therefore will allow you to work on tighter margins and make money from products and sales those who sell just "a little" can't.

If you are already selling on the Amazon platform than all you need to do is convert to a business account and ask them to enrol you in Fulfillment by Amazon. It doesn't cost anything to sign up so you can just try it and see how you get on.

Tip. When you sign up to Fulfilment by Amazon with Amazon.com you can only sell things within the US. Which strikes me as a bit odd, seeing as how the Internet is supposed to be a global way of doing business. You can sell using Fulfillment by Amazon in some of the other countries Amazon operates in - Germany, France, UK and Japan - but you need to sign up with them separately. Initially you probably wouldn't want to do this but it could be a way of expanding in future.

Chapter 2 : Private Label Rights Market Research

Even though you're skipping over the grunt work with the private label products (while everyone else must slave away), there's still one vital step you must perform just like everybody else.

You need to research the markets you move into, so you can understand the customers in those markets.

You may wonder, "Why is this step important since the product and sales copy are already done for you with a private label rights products?"

Well, first of all, this doesn't mean that you have to read a million books or spend countless days researching the subject.

But, it you do need to get "in tune" with who you're selling to. Another way of putting it is you must be able to relate your customers (as though you were "one of them").

The reason is because when you can speak your customers language and know the "conversation going on in their mind," then you always know what else to offer them. Plus, it's easy to tell them about your products in way that makes them sell like hotcakes!

An example of not doing this is an athletic person who's never experienced the struggle of being overweight moving into the weight loss market.

This person is not likely to understand why someone overweight just doesn't "stop overeating and not exercising."

It's simple, right?

However, this is not how your customers (usually) think of their problem. To them it's probably caused by genetics. They can't imagine giving up many of their favorite foods, and exercise seems dreadful.

How do you think they're going to react if you simply tell them that it's their fault?

You're going to lose a lot of sales by not empathizing with your customer's plight and addressing what's going in his or her mind. Just like his or her just like a good friend would. Moreover, you'll never be able to create products your customers desire if you don't do this.

An example of somebody doing this very thing right for this market is Richard Simmons (the energetic weight-loss guru). He was once overweight and he knows exactly what his customers are thinking and feeling.

He can authentically relate from his own past experiences.

Now, keep in mind, that the weight loss market is not unique. For every market, your customers are having a unique conversation going on that you must identify with in order to profit.

So, how do you uncover this conversation, especially if you're the athletic person who's never experienced being overweight?

Here are 3 simple ways:

1. Take an afternoon trip to the bookstore and go through all of the magazines your customers are reading. For example, if your market is composed of brides-to-be, then

look at all of the wedding magazines. Pay close attention to the headlines, sub-headlines and images on the front cover. If there are no magazines for the topic, see what books are being sold on that topic at Amazon.com. You can also search BarnesandNobles.com to see which books are selling well enough to be found inside their store.

2. Watch infomercials on TV that address the topic and go through study direct-response copy. See HardToFindAds.com and top sellers at Clickbank.com for ads. Look at your competitors sales copy and see what points they're addressing. Do all of your competitors address a specific point above all others in their headlines?

3. Read and ask questions on forums. If you don't experience snoring in your relationship

(and you're selling a product on how to end snoring), then talk to couples that do. What problems do they all share? What do they talk about? Their insight may just be the information you need for a million dollar business, product, or promotion! Don't hesitate to ask a lot of questions and listen to what they have to say.

Steps for private labelling on Amazon

Research and Select a Product

This is arguably the most important and time-consuming step in the process, but the friendly folks at Amazon lighten the burden a bit by pointing you in the right direction.

That's because the site releases detailed lists of their best-selling products. While the lists are designed to give consumers a chance to see what's popular, you can use them to your advantage, too.

The best-seller rankings essentially serve as your pre-market product research. Instead of developing a product and then testing to see if it sells well, you can start by seeing if the product sells well and then make a decision regarding whether or not you want to pursue it.

When mining Amazon's top-100 rankings for each category, be on the lookout for items that are lightweight, high-ranking and generic.

Generic refers to something like a water bottle, silicone spatula or flashlight — all items that can easily be produced with your own brand and packaging. In other words, you wouldn't want to select a product that's brand-driven — such as an iPhone or Nike running shoes — because those are protected products that can't be private labeled.

Once you find a product that you're interested in, it's time for phase two of the product research stage.

Check Out the Competition

During this phase, study your competition to see how they're doing.

For example, let's say the product you've honed in on is an insulated water bottle. While you may know from the top-100 rankings one insulated water bottle brand sells well, you need to learn more about the competitive landscape.

Using the search box at the top of Amazon, run a query for "insulated water bottle" and review the results.

Open up the first five listings and record the following information in a spreadsheet: price, number of reviews, Amazon best-sellers rank and quality of listing. The latter point is discretionary, but after doing some research, you'll quickly be able to tell the difference between a good listing and a bad one.

Using the information you gather from these five listings, which serve as your sample of the marketplace, determine whether the opportunity is worth pursuing.

Ideally, you want to see the following in your spreadsheet:

- An average price point between $10 and $40
- Low numbers of reviews (though a higher number isn't a deal-breaker)

- The majority of the best-sellers ranks below 1,000
- Average or low-quality listings

Don't be afraid if you can't find a product right away. It usually takes me hours of research to find an opportunity I believe will work.

However, let's say your research for insulated water bottles met all of these requirements. Now you're ready to find a supplier.

Find and Contact a Supplier

Once you know you have a good product opportunity, it's time to find a supplier.

While it's possible — depending on the product — you could find a supplier in the U.S., it's highly unlikely that you'll find a cost-effective one. Trust me on this one and head over to Alibaba to look for an international supplier.

Start your supplier search by entering the same key phrase into the Alibaba search box. In this case, a simple search of "insulated water bottle" will give you thousands of different products and suppliers.

Find the style you're looking for and research a few different suppliers. Depending on how thorough their listings are, you can usually see the required minimum order quantity (MOQ), price range, style options, lead time and whether they allow for private labeling. However, you'll need to email the supplier to get an accurate quote for your order.

I've found suppliers are willing to negotiate, even on your first order. While they may claim their MOQ is 500 or 1,000 units, it's entirely possible to talk them down to, say, 250 or 300 units.

Generally, there's also room for negotiating prices. Just act confident and pretend you've been there before — even if you haven't!

Get Your Logo, Design and Packaging

To save time and streamline the process, you can often work on step three alongside step two.

Once you've found a supplier who's willing to let you private label the product, you have to choose your marketing materials. Don't worry, though — you don't have to create them yourself!

Use a website like Fiverr or Upwork to hire a professional designers at competitive prices.

On Fiverr, you simply search for the designers and then send them your job proposal. On Upwork (formerly Elance), you'll actually create a project proposal and have designers bid for your project.

Assuming you've had time to develop a brand name during this process, you'll want your designer to create a logo that represents your brand and vibrant packaging that sets it apart from your competitors — the ones listed in your spreadsheet from step one.

Once you have your design files, send them over to your supplier and tell them to proceed with your order.

Craft a Compelling Listing

Depending on your supplier's lead time, you could wait anywhere from 10 to 30 days for your shipment to arrive.

Use this time wisely. Start by focusing on your listing. Follow Amazon's directions and protocol for creating a seller account and then create a listing for your product.

To create a compelling listing:

- Use high quality images
- Clearly explain how the product works
- Describe why it's valuable
- Highlight what sets it apart from the competition

While you'll have to work within the constraints of what Amazon does and does not allow on listings, you should be able to use bolded text and bullet points to accentuate key facts.

As you likely noticed during step one, many sellers don't do a good job with their listings, yet still sell well. Can you imagine how many more units they would sell with descriptive listings?

This is your chance to set your product apart and differentiate your brand as knowledgeable and informative.

Use Fulfillment by Amazon to Create Passive Income

Some of you are probably saying, "This whole process doesn't sound like passive income."

Well, up until now, you may be right. However, assuming you did a thorough job in the previous steps, you're almost ready to sit back and reap the benefits.

Thanks to the Fulfillment by Amazon (FBA) program, you don't have to manage the monotony of picking, packing and shipping orders.

While FBA takes a small percentage of your profits, it's well worth it for most sellers. Your shipping costs are included in the fees and your products automatically become eligible for free Prime shipping, which could help you make more sales.

Plus, FBA sellers often enjoy higher search rankings than non-FBA sellers. While Amazon hasn't officially confirmed this, I've noticed it with my own products and friends have seen similar benefits.

For detailed information on how to setup an FBA listing, how it works, pricing, success stories, and more, check out Amazon's guide for getting started.

Once you set up your listing and ship your products to the distribution center, you can be as hands-off as you'd like. When a customer makes a purchase, you don't even have to lift a finger. Amazon's fulfillment centers take care of everything, including returns and customer service issues.

Make Your First Sale

In any business or industry, the first sale is typically the hardest to make. You don't have a reputation or any existing customers, so it can be challenging to convince someone to purchase your product.

Many sellers run some sort of sale or discount during a product's launch. By reducing the price, you lower the customer's perceived risk and entice them to take a chance on your product.

You can also use Amazon's internal advertising system, which allows you to pay for your product to be listed in relevant on-site searches. This is a great way to increase visibility and attract an initial burst of sales.

Another option is to use Google AdWords to drive traffic to your listing. While AdWords will be more expensive, I tend to generate more sales from it than from other methods.

While these are the most common strategies, there are hundreds of other ways to increase sales and traffic. This is where you can get creative and have fun with your product!

Or, if everything is working on its own, simply sit back and let the passive income accumulate.

Best Private Label Products to Sell on Amazon

There is a LOT of people with a lot of money being that made by people who has selling private lebel products to sell on the platform of Amazon.

Now that selling private label products on Amazon has become so popular, it's interesting to see what people think are good products to build a brand around. There are some who reach for the stars and build complicated items that cost a lot of money to produce, while others go the simple route.

Also can Promote your Products

Marketing on Amazon refers to a relationship to your business, in which you can business online or promote your business online or the sites that can promote your products of a Amazon.

The websites which you can promote your business, provide you a service on marketing, and the channels customers to the direct through a link on web, text ad or banner ad on the site. From the Amazon, if the customer buys your product, the affiliate owner of the website also receives a commission but it has a big benefit that your product is sale and also you got reviews. As an affiliate marketer, to optimize your earning potential and you must be able to select the best of your products for your affiliate website.

Why are you private labeling?

I think the best way to start any endeavor is to ask yourself why. Why are you creating a private label product in the first place? I would venture to say that most people who are trying to create their own brand on Amazon are doing so because they are tired of running around from store to store doing retail arbitrage, or spending hours online trying to find products they can flip from eBay to Amazon and so on.

Let's face it, reselling sucks... Sure it's great for some quick cash, but the fact that there's never any stable and consistent income without putting it in a lot of time can be very difficult.

Most people see private label products as an opportunity to provide consistency in revenue as well as a means to cut down on overall labor.

While folks definitely understand and see the benefits of building your own brand when it comes to not having to constantly find new products in order to make revenue, there is one thing that keeps them from being successful with private label products... Over complication.

We think that the more complex the item, and the more work that's put into the item, translates to the more revenue generating capability it has. Sure, and iPad is going to have much more value than a plastic cup, but building the next iPad does not guarantee that anybody is going to buy it.

There are far more people making tons of money with simple items then there are those that produce complex products in the private label space.

The simpler the better

When it comes to the best private label products to sell on Amazon, the simpler the better. There are a few rules that I have when it comes to products that I brand myself. It's not rocket science, but it works:

- **Is the item Evergreen?** Meaning, will someone buy this product over and over again (for example, people will always buy shampoo. When they run out, they will buy more shampoo.)
- **Are people actually searching for your kind of product?** Imagine spending thousands of dollars on your own branded product only to find out that

nobody is even looking for it. I don't mean that they aren't searching for your specific brand, I mean that they aren't even looking for your type of product. The easiest way to test what people are looking for prior to spending a lot of time and money on product id to do keyword research on Amazon. You can do this by manually typing in keywords into the Amazon search bar to see if people are searching for that word, or you can use software. There are a lot of tools out there that just automatically use the Amazon suggestion bar to come up with ideas, and that sort of works, but I prefer Keyword Inspector or KIPRT because the former lets you do reverse ASIN searching that tells you exactly what customers searched for when the went to a particular listing, and the latter gives you a ton of data that lets you find gaps in the market that you can take advantage of. The reverse ASIN searching doesn't just rely on keywords that's in the listing too... for example, if you are looking at a bulldozer toy some of the keywords that Keyword Inspector brings up might be something like "construction toys for kids" even though it might not be in the listing at all. It's really powerful.

- **Does the item have a lot of competition?** You'd be surprised that there are still a ton of items that don't have a lot of competition. On top of that, even if your product has "competition" are you able to easily make multiples that you can use to make new listings that your competition can't?

- **Is the item simple and cheap to produce?** Like I said before you don't need to build the next iPad. I'd rather sell 20 units of plastic cup bundles a day at $24.99 each than one iPad at $299 with a very low profit margin.
- **Does the item have proven sales data against it?** Have I tested the listing that I created on Amazon with products that I found at retail stores first before I made a decision to buy in bulk? A lot of people miss this step, which is probably the most important, because it proves whether or not your product is actually going to sell prior to you spending a lot of money sourcing from a manufacturer

That's it. Like I said, it's not rocket science. The best private label products to sell on Amazon are those that are simple, Evergreen, and have proven sales data. Doing private label this way allows you to rinse and repeat easily. The more that you do it the more assets you build for yourself in the long run. A really easy way to get private label product ideas quickly by people that create and manage private label products for a living is through a site called MooFlip. They have vendors that do online arbitrage, Merch by Amazon done for you designs, and done for your private label product research. It's a great way to save a ton of time researching private label products to sell on Amazon and just get them handed to you.

Chapter 3 : How Much Could You Earn With a Private-Label Business?

Since different types of products have different price points and associated costs, these numbers are estimates. However, here's an idea of your potential earnings.

Products that rank within the top 100 in their category often bring in thousands of dollars per day in revenue. Products that rank in the top 500 typically produce hundreds of dollars per day. Even a product in the top 2,000 to 3,000 can earn you a steady supplemental income.

While it's difficult to estimate the initial investment for your own private-label brand, since it depends on your product, I can give you an idea of how much I spent on my first one, a basic grilling accessory.

I ordered 500 units at a per-unit cost of $3.20. In addition to the $1,600 cost of initial inventory, I spent around $400 to design my packaging and logo, start a website, set up my Amazon business account and pay other minor expenses. So launching my first private-label brand cost me about $2,000.

However, I know people who spent only a few hundred dollars getting their first brand off the ground — and also people who spent many thousands.

Look for a healthy profit margin. I like to aim for a per-unit profit margin of at least 50%. It all depends on the product, but there's a niche for every budget.

While there's a lot of information in this comprehensive guide. Dig around, do some research, speak with other sellers and find out what else you can do to make your private-labeling business a successful and lucrative endeavor.

Your Turn: Will you try launching a private-labeling business? If you've sold private-labeled products, we'd love to hear about your experience!

Some lucrative Amazon FBA Private Label Product Ideas

Finding an Amazon FBA product can be very difficult! Here are profitable products people are selling that I believe are worth exploring for additional opportunities.

List of Potential Amazon FBA Niches/Products:

- Neoprene Camera Bags
- Neoprene Bibs
- Knife Sharpener

- Alarm Clocks
- Flashlight
- Bike Light
- LED Lantern
- Decals for Self Balancing Scooters
- Bluetooth Waterproof Speakers
- Mosquito Repellent Bracelets
- Cell Phone Camera Lens Attachment
- Phone Screen Protector
- Hammocks
- Kinesiology Tape
- Picture Frames

Two secret of sourcing for private product ideas

Idea 1 – Go to review websites and look at what other people are selling and looking for reviews on and reverse engineer your own slightly unique angle!

Idea 2 – Other great resources for finding profitable products to sell is website selling marketplaces. The strategy is to find websites that are selling a lot of private lable products and use that as market validation that private label products will sell in that space! Here are 2 great sources to find websites selling Amazon Affiliate products where you can then identify if you could make a Private Label FBA entry into the space:

1. Flippa.com

2. EmpireFlippers.com

How To Find Suppliers & Manufacturers Fast

Finding wholesale suppliers and manufacturers is actually quite easy. You can begin to find many in a matter of minutes. However, what you'll find the most challenging part is making sure that they're the right fit for you. Here's the steps that I follow below:

1. Have A List Of Potential Products You Want To Sell

It's important to make sure you have a list of potential products that you want to sell. I recommend having at least 10, as you're going to learn quickly when you start talking to suppliers that some products you might have had your hopes on simply might not work.

You can't be too attached to selling one particular product on Amazon. Just because you might think it's the best product for you to sell, there are many other factors that will go into making a decision to sell it on Amazon, just make sure you have a list of products that meet my criteria for selling on Amazon.

2. Search For Suppliers & Manufacturers For That Product

For each product, you're going to search online for potential suppliers and the manufacturers for that product that are already making it. This will allow you to private label the product easily and inexpensively.

To sell on Amazon now that you've found a product to sell that is must profitable and ensured you to did the full proper research for that product, then you are now fully being ready to fine new manufactures and suppliers wholesale that can private label your product. For selling on Amazon this is the one of the most important steps for you, as you need to ensure you that you can must find the right product to sell and that it's quality is high, with a healthy and great profit margin.

I primarily use Google when I'm trying to find suppliers inside the United States. Some products you'll likely want to find USA suppliers, such as if you want to sell a food item or supplement.

To find suppliers on Google, I just search for the product keyword name and add "suppliers" or "private label" or "manufacturers" at the end of it.

For example, I'd search for "yoga mat suppliers" or "yoga mat private label" or "yoga mat manufacturers". This will come up with a list of companies all over the world that are making these products.

To find suppliers on Amazon, I just do a search for the keyword "yoga mat" or whatever the product is that I want to sell. You'll then see many, many companies appear that are making that product, along with some valuable information.

You want to make sure that the suppliers on Amazon are assessed and verified, as this will ensure you're picking the most reputable suppliers and that you don't fall into trouble later.

3. Contact The Potential Suppliers & Manufacturers

The next step on how to find suppliers is to reach out to them and contact them.

Find a company or product you like? Then talk to them to get more details.

How you communicate with suppliers is very important. You don't want to sound like a newbie to private labeling a product, but rather a big company that knows what they're doing. This is because they don't want to deal with newbies, they want serious buyers that they believe will build a long-term relationship with them and spend a lot of money.

So make sure you're formal and professional when communicating with suppliers.

What do you ask these suppliers? What info do you want to find out?

Well, there's a lot. Some that I like to find out is:

- What is the minimum order quantity?
- What quote can you give me on 500 units, 1000 units, 5000 units, etc...?
- Tell me more about the product, how it's made, the quality of it, what makes it different from others, etc...
- Tell me more about the company that makes it, your manufacturing process,

what makes you different from others, etc…
- What is the size and weight of the product?
- What will it cost 1000 units to ship to USA?
- What is the turnaround time if I order today?
- Do you allow private labelling? Do you put the label on the product or packaging? How much will that cost each unit?
- What kind of labeling or packaging options do you have?

Those are just some of the questions you'd ask a potential supplier, just to gather as much info as possible.

You'd want to get as much information as possible, from all suppliers, so that you can make the best decision on which company to choose to private label your product with.

What you'll find is that all suppliers with offer a different price and details, so you need to weigh the pros and cons for each supplier.

It's also important to pick a supplier that has good communication and you can build a good long-term relationship with, as you'll likely be working with this supplier for the long-term.

4. Choose A Supplier Or Manufacturer To Private Label Your Product

Once you've done all the research and determined the best supplier for you, then it's time to place an order.

I personally have always started with at least 1000 units of a product, however with many suppliers you can start with as low as 100 units. It depends on the supplier and your own personal budget.

One risk to starting with a low number of units is that if you potentially run out of stock selling on Amazon, then it can hurt your rankings for your Amazon listing. So you want to make sure that you're always in stock at all times and have enough inventory.

Usually suppliers will request a wire transfer, in which case you'll have to get the details from them and make the payment through your bank. Others might accept a credit card or PayPal.

Once you've placed your order and are waiting for your product to get made ready, you'll want to focus on creating your label and design for your product so that you can send that to the supplier to put on it.

Chapter 4 : Uses and usefulness of private

Private label for the wholesaler apparel manufactured solely. It doesn't have to complete head to head with name brands.

You can deal directly with your sources and suppliers.

The private branding, you can create your own unique image, which begets identity of marketing and also promotes stronger customer loyalty and recognition.

Marketing and business tool

Retailers have extended the concept of private label to identify a brand with a store, a concept known as the "store brand". This can be far more profitable than selling nationally advertised brands. To illustrate, a Food Marketing Institute study in the United States found that retailers earn a 35% gross margin on store-branded products compared to 25.9% on comparable nationally advertised brands.

Outsourcing

Several corporations source products from specialized manufacturers, which may or may not own their brands, as establishing their own production facilities would require substantial investments in equipment, human resources, and patents. Sourcing from a specialized company that has already made such investments with spare production capacity may be a viable alternative. If the two companies find that the market situation allows to avoid or minimize direct competition without stealing each other's market share (cannibalization), then both companies may find an agreement whereby the specialized manufacturer supplies the goods to the other. The methods to reduce cannibalization are general marketing practices such as dedicated distribution channels, different image and customer perception of the brands, pricing, and separate regional presences. The same basic concepts apply to the service industry (e.g., customer services helplines).

Market entry

Private labels may be behind the decision of some companies to enter the market with products that are quite different, but somehow associable, to those that have made them famous (e.g., apparel companies launching perfumes, car companies launching watches). Private labels may be extremely profitable for companies with a dominant market share and for certain products that enjoy high customer recognition.

Safety and quality

As sophisticated technologies become widespread (and even subsidized) in emerging countries, sourcing of a wide range of products can be made at very low cost. These same products may have prices that allow for net margins to account up to several times the cost of the goods sold. Customers may be unaware of this business practice and may be paying higher prices for products that differ little from others with less famous brands. On the other hand, some companies do provide additional guarantees to these products offering better quality, customer support, and additional services.

Private label products are generally sold in many countries, so it is essential that all products are of high quality and comply with all the relevant single or global market standards, including sustainability and environmental impacts. This can be done by performing certification and audits, inspections, hygiene monitoring, and testing of food, beverages, and packaging.

Use by small companies

The use of private-label products by small companies has grown. Small companies usually do not have any input in the recipes or packaging of the products they buy. They buy from a specialty food company that uses their recipes and simply label for the individual retail store. Small companies do this for advertising benefits. For example, if John's Farm Market sells jams or salsas, each time the consumer uses the product they are reminded of their visit to John's Farm Market, where they will have to return to repurchase it. The brand also benefits when products are gifted, as this allows the gift recipient to become another potential customer. In recent years, Amazon has been a popular channel for small companies to launch a private label product, where almost 500k products are released on a daily basis, many of which are private label products. By leveraging Amazon FBA infrastructure, small companies can launch private label brands without having to invest into any storing facilities.

Private Label Categories

Almost every consumer product category has both branded and private label offerings, including:

- Personal care
- Beverages
- Cosmetics
- Paper products
- Household cleaners
- Condiments and salad dressings
- Dairy items

unique brand for retailers. Retailers with pretty good private-label brands will be able to create better sales opportunities for themselves. They can build value and recognition from the customers. Private-brand products allow retailers to differentiate their products from competitors' products, and provide consumers with an alternative to other brands.

Disadvantages of private labelled products

- The disadvantages of adding a private label line are few, as long as you have the financial resources to invest in developing such a product. The main disadvantages include:
- Manufacturer dependency - Since production of your product line is in the hands of a third-party manufacturer, it's important to partner with well-

established companies. Otherwise, you could miss out on opportunities if your manufacturer runs into problems.

- Difficulty building loyalty - Established household brands have the upper hand and can often be found in a variety of retail outlets. Your product will only be sold in your stores, limiting customer access to it. Of course, limited availability could also be an advantage, giving customers a reason to come back and buy from you.

Although private label products are typically sold at a lower price point than their name brand brethren, some private label brands are now being positioned as premium products, with the higher price tag to prove it.

Conclusion

Thank you again for buying this book!

I hope this book was able to help you to start fulfilling your dreams.

The next step is to take action on all what you have read and see the amazing change in your business.

Finally, if you enjoyed this book, then I'd like to ask you for a favor, would you be kind enough to leave a review for this book on Amazon? It'd be greatly appreciated!

Thank you and good luck!

Best Regards,

Braden Nardelli

www.ingramcontent.com/pod-product-compliance
Lightning Source LLC
Chambersburg PA
CBHW061444180526
45170CB00004B/1557